TREASURE Y

BY

CHERISHING YOUR SPOUSE

SUZANNE E. UZZELL

Treasure Your Marriage

By

Cherishing Your Spouse

A Gift For: _____

From: _____

Date: _____

Treasure Your Marriage

By

Cherishing Your Spouse

Paper Back ISBN: 978-1-329-71117-4

Dedications

I thank God for allowing me to write this book he has inspired me in many ways to remind the Christian Marriages to treasure the gift he gave to them. The marriage relationship is dear to Gods heart because he created the Marriage union.

I dedicate this book to my husband Jahi J. Uzzell whom I love dearly and stand in love with. I thank God for allowing us to come together grow and share what he has given us.

This book is also dedicated to Christian Marriages who will develop and grow within their union. I pray this book will encourage Godly marriages to prosper, be restored as they learn how to grow together in God and in love.

CONTENTS

TREASURE YOUR MARRIAGE

Treasure Your Marriage

There are hidden treasures
I placed within your marriage
that will take you time to see
as you spend days, months and years together
you will learn how to operate in and appreciate
this beautiful relationship that I
hold dear to me and gave to thee.

I have gifted you with this treasure here on earth
the one I have created, designed and re-birthed.
I want you to cherish the one I placed by your side
but remember to always let me be your guide.

Never forget to show my love, the love
that is from Heaven above.
My love is unconditional, patient and kind
my love will guide you through the test of time.
My love will bind your hearts together as one.

Treasure your marriage by cherishing your spouse

If I was writing a general letter to spouses about marriage I would begin by saying welcome to your union of love where God intended you to be there are many hidden treasures you will find in your mate so cherish the journey where you will explore many new things about your significant other that you never saw on the bare surface.

God wants you to begin searching and not just be complacent with who you think your husband/wife is he wants to develop you to find the beautiful treasure that lies hidden within you and what is hidden within them.

There is great value in our Marriage relationship and if we are not careful we can devalue or disregard it. We must recognize the treasure of this relationship and realize it has great worth.

Treasure your marriage by cherishing your spouse

The value potential is much greater than silver and gold and it yields greater profit because it is an investment of a lifetime.

When we look at the word treasure it means to regard or treat as precious: cherish, great value and highly priced. When we treasure someone we learn to cherish the person hold them in high regard and place a great value on that person or relationship.

We know the worth and value of that person. When we cherish someone we hold and treat them as dear, we feel love for them and care for that person.

God has given us hidden treasure in our marriage union and he wants us to cherish our spouse by loving them in order to do that we must allow God to love through us.

Treasure your marriage by cherishing your spouse

We must also learn how to value our spouses, not devalue them or the marriage relationship.

God wants us to learn how to serve each other in love. We must also learn how to be happy and fulfilled with the choice we have chosen and that is our significant other our spouse that God blessed us with.

When you are happy with your choice you become content with your spouse and your union. You are not sidetracked by other desires that are not healthy to your union. God wants to settle us in our marriage union there are so many couples that are not settled in their marriage. When you are settled you are not stagnated, swayed or easily moved.

Treasure your marriage by cherishing your spouse

No matter what you may experience whether unusual circumstances or life oppositions you will be able to work together and remain committed because you are settled in the marriage and also dedicated to one another and your relationship.

God wants us to grow in him and also together, he wants us to grow in love with one another.

There are many positive and negative life experiences a marriage union will face we were designed by God to endure the hardships, enjoy the beauty of creating shared memories, experience joy and bask in the fun but also pull together and work as a team through the difficult moments that tests our union from time to time.

Treasure your marriage by cherishing your spouse

We can grow and become stronger if we value the tests that are set before us.

We can cherish our spouse in the greatest of times and also in the times of facing adversity and hardship. We can become a victorious team built to last no matter what we experience together. It is how we face these day to day life experiences that will determine our outcome.

There are so many Christian marriages that are ending in divorce because they never had the opportunity to grow together and flourish and see the value of their marriage. They face various differences and are easily swayed to end it when they can't come to resolve or resolution.

Some individuals came in the union with an ideal of fantasy how they think marriage would or should be. Some have the fantasy that being in love was all you need to remain happy and together.

You never have to nurture or work through issues in the relationship as they occur. This fantasy causes blindness and creates a false sense of belief that romance only or the emotional state of being in love is all you need to stay together and remain happy. They welcome the blissful feeling only and draw away or dismiss the realities that come along with being married.

I challenge this false belief by saying once we walk in covenant relationship after we said our vows we are called by God to stand in love not fall out of love.

There is no such thing as the love has died in my opinion. However I agree with the statement two people can grow apart or be indifferent but Gods love never grows cold or dies. We must admit if God placed his spirit within us and we are children of God then we also have the capacity to allow God to love through us.

We must surrender ourselves to God daily in order for this to be achieved in us and through us.

We can grow apart and also walk in disagreement this means we can walk in the spirit of disagreement with our spouse and this can cause us to see them in a different light just because we are walking in opposition instead of walking in agreement with them.

We can also embrace discord, anger, resentment and ungodly behaviors that will drive a wedge in between the spouse and eventually damage the relationship.

Treasure your marriage by cherishing your spouse

There are many devices that can pull people apart if allowed or if entertained. We must be careful to examine self and these negative behaviors and obstacles that can cause detriment to the marriage relationship.

We must learn to walk in the power and spirit of agreement. When we walk in agreement we make the decision to walk in unity. Christian marriages are called to a level of humility and dependency on Jesus Christ.

If you are going to walk in agreement it takes humbleness of heart, prayer, confession and submission toward Jesus and each other especially when you face situations where there is a difference of opinion.

Amos 3:3(KJV) Can two walk together, except they be agreed?

Treasure your marriage by cherishing your spouse

God calls us into a walk together and this requires for us to practice walking in the spirit of agreement. When you are in agreement you are operating in oneness.

Mark 10:8 And the two shall become one flesh, so that they are no longer two, but one flesh.

This is where God wants us because we are growing to become one. This means we are learning not to operate from an independent perspective when coming together. We should be developing and embracing the team concept, the unit and learn to become unified which takes lots of practice, preparation, persistence and prayer in order to adapt to this new way of living and functioning in the marriage relationship.

This is a process that is necessary to build the team because I is not found in team so we must function and develop together instead of apart.

With that said we must be reminded that walking in the spirit of agreement will not alleviate the relationship from facing opposition and we can also agree to disagree.

God has designed the man and woman with different thinking capacities when he created us. We think differently and are also shaped by different life experiences which may cause us to handle situations in various ways that are contrary to one another.

We are also conditioned by our parental upbringing in childhood along with our own pattern of thinking which shapes the way we see things and handle them. However in the marriage union we are challenged to congregate and fuse ideas and concepts and create new practices that will be great for the family dynamics.

God has created us to collaborate together and it is okay to come to the table with different ideas and difference of opinion but he wants us to leave the table with great concepts and proper communication that will inspire both people to work as a team.

We achieve this by seeking him in prayer for godly wisdom and discipline every time we kick against rocks and rough edges in our union.

When you make the decision to walk in agreement it means you are always on the same page operating in the same spirit. When we seek God for his counsel, guidance, wisdom and discipline he will help us to achieve this growth in our relationship. Let us come to the conclusion there is a lot of great work that takes place in order to cultivate and grow the love that will maintain the relationship.

We must not operate in fantasy but in reality when we function in our relationship and we must view it the way God views it.

This is an excellent work God has called us into after all this is what we signed up for when we said I do. However it is regretful that some of us didn't get the memo of what the true marriage union would be like. All we knew was we truly loved our spouse and we couldn't wait to get married to them.

While we were in preparation someone should have told us or shared with us that marriage is a beautiful union designed by God that requires our daily participation and undivided attention. This relationship is one of the most important relationships that can affect our life in a positive or negative way.

Marriage should not be entered into lightly because there is a special price both spouses will pay but the end results will be beautiful if we would allow God to work on our behalf and if we see the treasures he placed in our spouse and they also see the treasures God placed in us.

There is a great value that we sometimes overlook on a daily basis. The marriage relationship brings oneness that God intended for us to experience. If we learn how to function in this oneness it would be very beneficial to the union.

Most of the time we can function from a dysfunctional point of view where we think the relationship is thriving so we continue to let things be and it becomes chaotic.

God wants to bring us to a functional and extraordinary relationship. He will bring order and structure this is where God can get glory out of our relationship when we allow him to change our way of thinking and methods that are not working.

God wants to restore order in our homes and within us. He wants us to serve him and one another not from a place of obligation but serve out of love.

Love one another
as
I have
loved you.

JOHN 13:34

Treasure your marriage by cherishing your spouse

When we learn to cherish our spouse then we will love to assist them, care for them, pray for them, and value them.

God wants us to be happy with our choice not murmur or complain or be unhappy. When we look at why we wanted to marry our spouse then we can experience what were the characteristics, values, traits we admired and liked about them.

There are many stages in the marriage relationship and we must learn and understand these in order for us to understand how we grow. It is a process our relationship goes through here are seven stages I list that God revealed to me for us to view.

~ 7 Stages of Marriage Growth ~

Stage 1~ Still Getting to know each other

We were and will always be playing the getting to know you game because we are always evolving, changing and rediscovering ourselves and our soul mate. As we grow in our relationship there will be new ways we connect and reconnect.

Stage 2~ Becoming comfortable around one another.

Learning how to relax, relate and be yourself and allow your spouse to have liberty to be themselves is crucial and key to being comfortable.

It also takes time to get into a couple rhythm and pattern in your marriage and with each other. It is a process that you evolve into as you spend more time with one another.

Stage 3~ Learning how to operate as a team.

You are on the same team therefore you must have the same goals and objectives in your relationship. In order to grow as one you must learn each other's strengths, weaknesses and learn how to strategize and operate together in various capacities in order to achieve victories in the union.

Learning how to collaborate, share idea, and work as a team is necessary and important to grow together in the union when we continue to put these ideals into practice our team will become better.

Treasure your marriage by cherishing your spouse

Stage 4~ Sharpening your tools – Communication, friendship, intimacy, compatibility, faithfulness etc

In your marriage you will always need to sharpen your tools, work at building up yourself and your relationship. When you strengthen your skills your marriage becomes strengthened. There are many ways to do so.

Explore your options in finding ways to sharpen your tools and you will experience great results.

Stage 5 ~ Enduring & redeveloping the marriage relationship as we redevelop ourselves.

Learning how to endure in your marriage is a beautiful commitment that will lead you to resolve every time you want to give up or quit. There are times we must redevelop and revamp the relationship and our self. This is normal activity and work that is necessary in order to achieve newness and development within ourselves and in the union.

Stage 6 ~ Making the necessary adjustment in order to serve one another and live peaceably with one another.

There are a lot of adjustments we make as individuals and as a couple in our marriage relationship. We will always make adjustments as we learn to walk together. Life is all about adjusting and adapting to change.

In order for us to serve one another we must learn to adjust our thinking and give our spouse what is required and that is our love, devotion, and concern.

Treasure your marriage by cherishing your spouse

God calls us to live in peace with one another, this peace is developed through prayer and understanding our spouse.

Because Jesus is the Prince of Peace it must also be received from him first. We must also have inner peace and tranquility in order to share peace in our relationship. We must also learn how to be at peace when things are not always peaceful.

This is another work that must be practiced. We must be patient with ourselves and our spouse because we will miss the mark but the lesson is to develop an atmosphere of understanding and mercy in your relationship.

When we come to a place of acceptance of self and each other the greater peace we obtain in the union.

Stage 7~ Growing in love with God and each other ~ Growing in your faith

In our marriage relationship God continues to call us unto him and each other. We learn to grow in love with Jesus first in order to grow in love with our spouse.

When we receive and experience the love of Jesus everyday he will love through us as we spend time in his presence we will be able to share what he has given us. God wants us to grow in love and also grow in faith.

As we share with one another our belief we are learning to walk in faith and in agreement with God for our lives and our union. We are called to build each other up in the faith and grow together.

When we understand these seven stages of marriage growth we will learn our purpose within the marriage union and we will have a better understanding of how the marriage union functions and what's the role we play in it. We must continue to put these stages into practice and we are reminded of the work we must value and strive to do every day.

We must place great value on our marriage relationship and when we do that we are choosing to honor our vows. This is the Godly covenant we entered into with our soul mate. The vows are significant and God intended for us to submit and surrender to them.

The Vows also reveal to us what we need to do and what we will experience in the union.

Treasure your marriage by cherishing your spouse

Love, honor, cherish our spouse for better for worse ~ in sickness in health ~ rich or poor till death do us part. The vows are serious and we ought to abide by what we confessed when we got married. We will make mistakes but we must be committed to our commitment by remaining loyal.

With that said let us revisit the day we got married. Take a look at this vow exercise fill in the blank with your name and your spouse name and read aloud and commit to it daily.

FOR THIS REASON
a Man
WILL LEAVE HIS
FATHER AND MOTHER
AND BE UNITED TO
his Wife,
AND THEY WILL
BECOME ONE FLESH.
GENESIS 2:24

Treasure your marriage by cherishing your spouse

Question of Intent

Bride

_____, will you have this man to be your husband; to live together in the covenant of marriage? Will you love him, comfort him, honor and keep him, in sickness and in health; and, forsaking all others, be faithful to him as long as you both shall live?

Groom

_____, will you have this woman to be your wife; to live together in the covenant of marriage? Will you love her, in sickness and in health; and, forsaking all others, be faithful to her as long as you both shall live?

Treasure your marriage by cherishing your spouse

~ Vows ~

Groom

In the name of Jesus, I_____ take you, _____ to be my Wife, to have and to hold from this day forward, for better for worse, for richer for poorer, in sickness and in health, to love and cherish, until we are parted by death. This is my solemn vow.

~ Vows ~

Bride

In the name of Jesus, I_____ take you, _____ to be my Husband, to have and to hold from this day forward, for better for worse, for richer for poorer, in sickness and in health, to love and cherish, until we are parted by death. This is my solemn vow.

Treasure your marriage by cherishing your spouse

Songs of Solomon 3:4 I have found the one whom my soul loves.

Songs of Solomon 8:7 Many waters cannot quench love, either can the floods drown it: if a man would give all the substance of his house for love, it would utterly be contemned.

When you find the one your soul loves you will want to share your life with that person. Some people take a life time to finally find the one whom God has designed for them, when you find that gift you must learn how to love and be grateful you can experience this love that King Solomon is referring to. This is a precious love we must never take for granted.

Love never fails don't let your love grow cold because nothing can quench the flames that burns for one another. What God has joined together let no one put asunder.

Because God has joined you together you are one in him and he created the marriage union to show forth the relationship between Christ and the Church which is his (bride). God is preparing us in this marriage union.

He is purging us and working things out of us that are not like him. He is building our character within he is refining us that we may be like him. He is using our marriage as a ministry of love to heal us and others and to show forth his glory in the earth.

Treasure your marriage by cherishing your spouse

When we submit to God working in our marriage we are committed to the process. There is a process to molding and shaping. We must allow God to mold and shape us and our marriage relationship.

When you place value you are saying it's worth it, you begin to see the worth of your spouse, the worth of your relationship. When you see this worth you will begin to realize the importance of this relationship and what it brings or adds to your life.

There are times we overlook the value of its worth because we depreciate it over a period of time. Sometimes we are not aware we are doing this. It occurs in a subtle way at times.

When we don't pay attention to the signs of depreciation it can become hazardous to our

Treasure your marriage by cherishing your spouse

marriage. There are times we may take the relationship for granted or neglect its worth.

When we evaluate its true meaning then we will make better choices to protect and keep the relationship.

There is great worth in us and within our spouse and we must be able to see the jewels and pearls God placed within us and also within our spouse. When we recognize there is great treasure to behold we will uphold the relationship and learn how to guard one another because this union is priceless.

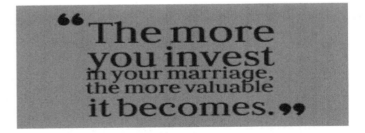

"The more you invest in your marriage, the more valuable **it becomes."**

CHERISH YOUR SPOUSE

Treasure your marriage by cherishing your spouse

When you care for something you will take care of it, maintain it, protect it, cherish it, hold close to you make sure it is taken care of when we care for people we hold them dear to our hearts; we want to bless them, share with them, make sure they are okay. You are concerned and devoted and you have great affection towards them.

God wants us to care for our spouses we must learn to take interest in there well being, hold them close and dear to our hearts. If we do this we will learn how to pray for them and encourage instead of discourage.

We will learn how to put them before ourselves in terms of service and devotion. We will be concerned about them in a healthy way.

Treasure your marriage by cherishing your spouse

We will have greater affection towards them and not be easily turned away from them even in their time of imperfections or shortcomings.

After all we also have imperfections and shortcomings that our spouses see in us because we are all human and we will fail each other from time to time. Our failure is not done intentionally towards one another but it is because of our humanness.

We thank God for his divine impartation of his spirit that dwells in us when we received him. God's spirit helps us to walk in him and teaches us how to love God, our self and others.

We should not judge our spouse's shortcomings or inconsistencies but we should humble ourselves and pray for them when they are struggling or fall short.

Our spouse in return should also do the same towards us. We must operate in God's grace and mercy and show that mercy towards one another just as God has and continues to show his grace and mercy towards us.

We all need to be saved from ourselves and the evil one and Jesus saves us every day. We must learn how to surrender ourselves, our lives and our marriage relationship over to the Lord and let him work the work in us and through us.

God wants to give the union new beginnings however it is up to us to see the opportunities of change and transformation that can restore and revive our relationship.

The marriage relationship always has hope and power to revitalize itself as long as the husband and wife are willing to see the potential within each other and in their relationship.

They must also have the willingness to embrace the challenges to start over again. God wants you to know you don't have to have a defeated relationship. Your relationship can prosper.

God wants us to move from defeat to restoration, from disgust to his grace, we must be willing to confess our faults, show mercy to one another and exercise God's grace in the areas of the relationship that needs it.

God intended for the husband and wife to grow together in love, unity, grace and in his power. There are times when we must confront the issues that plague the relationship before we confront we need to prayerfully seek godly council on how to begin conversing and what way we should be doing this. Much prayer is essential to move each other and the relationship forward.

The treasure that lies within us is the God given gifts he placed in us our treasure serves each other and has great purpose in the marriage.

Marriage is the mirror where we see ourselves daily, where we are in our marriage reveals a lot about our inner self and what we need to fine tune with in.

Marriage is a reflection of who you both are. The relationship reveals your strengths and weaknesses this mirror shows the beauty of the relationship and also the ugly what doesn't look so good in the relationship. The beauty must be embraced and the ugly must be erased.

Treasure your marriage by cherishing your spouse

The ugly represents the behaviors that are not pleasing to God or to each other, arguments that are not resolved in love, uncontrollable attitudes or abnormal behaviors that festers and turns you away from God and one another.

We must do away with selfishness, hardness of heart towards each other, resentment do to unresolved issues, unforgiveness, belittling each other, and all dysfunctional behaviors that don't edify the relationship.

If there is ugly in the relationship the beauty will not be seen because the ugly will overshadow the beauty. But there is beauty that is waiting to come forth the beauty is the Love that God released in both of your hearts for each other.

Treasure your marriage by cherishing your spouse

It is time to get back to the beauty, the love, kindness, joy, laughter, understanding, respect, resolving conflict the way God wants you to. Caring for your family, creating the atmosphere that is safe for the relationship to grow and thrive.

Understanding and sharing with each other all God wants you to give one other. This will bring you back to a beautiful place together.

It is time to be considerate of each other and learn how to be the mate God designed you to be, focus on your mandate as the mate – the husband – the wife that God is calling you to be, as you shift the focus off of your mate and onto yourself then you will be able to make the necessary changes and adjustments in your relationship.

Treasure your marriage by cherishing your spouse

Seek God to reveal to you what changes needs to be made and continue to pray and ask God to change whatever needs to be changed within you. There will be a lot of individual work that will be taking place within but it will strengthen the marriage relationship as a whole.

Don't be concerned about how much work needs to happen but begin the work by first submitting to God then accepting the changes that need to take place within you then focus only on your changes and your own inconsistent behaviors and shortcomings.

Learn how to celebrate your positive attributes you add to the relationship and continue to give that but begin to subtract the negative behaviors that are suffocating the relationship whatever that may be.

All relationships can have a positive return but it is the work you do that will make the outcome beautiful.

If you never work on self and the issues then you will not get a positive outcome you will continue to walk around the same issues for days which will turn into months and eventually years.

As a family you have the decision to make whether you want to experience victory in your marriage union or live with defeat. The enemy wants you to live in defeat and false emotions about each other but God knows that you can have the abundance of Joy and life in your marriage.

Treasure your marriage by cherishing your spouse

All you have to do is make the minor adjustments that will become major repairs and those repairs will last for years.

There is nothing wrong with having to identify and fix the repairs however the danger is when you don't know or acknowledge that there are repairs that need to be worked on because eventually whatever is not repaired will be detached and broken.

You don't want to live in brokenness because that is a place of being hurt, detached and in pain.

It is harder to put the pieces back together because there are so many parts that have been broken apart in the relationship.

Treasure your marriage by cherishing your spouse

There is nothing wrong with identifying the problems and working together to repair what was damaged.

Prayer can change the outcome of your marriage. If the repairs are overwhelming you can ask for help that is where therapy comes in or Christian or Pastoral counseling. You must determine where you are in terms of how much damage is done in the relationship and how the union can be repaired.

If you can't resolve the issues on your own through prayer, couple study of God's word and talking things out then there needs to be an intervention such as spiritual counseling that can determine the damage and the work that needs to be done in order to bring repairs in the union.

Never give up on your relationship no matter where you are and how you feel. Covenant is not a feeling but it is the agreement that you made to each other and to God.

God will honor your covenant. Learn how to surrender your marriage relationship back to God. Ask him to make the necessary changes that he wants to make and to add to your relationship what he wants to add.

God uses the relationship to build us up and also teach us many life lessons that improves and strengthens us. We must learn the many lessons within the marriage in order to grow inward, outward and spiritually.

We are not in the relationship just to be there or mark time we are here to workout, buildup, teardown self motives, create and transform our beings, our mind and ourselves. Our spouses will also partake in the same work. We will also experience sharing love, joy, peace, kindness and gentleness towards each other.

This is an ongoing work but the good news is two are better than one so we are working together as a team. God designed the union this way the Man and Woman complement each other and they both possess what the other one needs.

The woman assists and helps the man, she is his helpmeet and the man is the head of the woman he is assertive in leadership in a serving manner he operates in a servant hood leading style that she may follow his lead.

This leading is humbling self to follow Jesus by allowing him to guide him in all things great or small.

Proverbs 31:10-31 Excellent Wife ~She is the Crown of his head ~ Respects her husband ~ She tends to Business in and outside the home, is wise, does her husband good not evil all the days of her life.

Ephesians 5:22-29 Husband ~ He loves his wife as Christ loves the church. He gives of himself.

In essence the husband and wife submit to God and each other. God sees the marriage union as one team a family unit. It is in this family unit God wants to perform miracles, breathe into it, construct it, mold it, make it and shape it into his image because the earthly marriage is symbolic to the spiritual marriage between Christ and his bride the Church.

When we put a high price on our relationship and our spouse we will do everything possible to protect it from being damaged or discarded. God wants to give us a new perspective on how we are to view our spouse and our marriage relationship.

It is time to hold it in high regard and learn how to view it the way God views it.

As Christians God wants us to know that he designed the MARRIAGE INSTITUTION and this relationship must be unified even in a fallen world. Christian Marriage (Relationship) must not model the Worldly Marriage or relationship, God does honor all marriages in terms of heterosexual marriages, but the Christian Marriage is designed to reveal a greater Love which comes from God. God's love is unconditional and a Christian marriage learns to model the Love of God.

There is a process of denying self that must exist daily in order to achieve this in the relationship. The Marriage Union is a covenant that must be honored by the Husband and Wife and this Covenant is honored by God.

When vows was exchanged on the wedding day it wasn't just for that day but these vows shared was stating whether it was good times or bad, whether you have great health or poor health, whether your wealth status was rich at its best or poor at its worse nothing would break this covenant relationship except death.

Death was the only outcome that was the criteria to separate the marriage union, however because of disagreements or conflict people take it upon themselves to separate, divorce and break the vows and covenant. The first institution of Marriage God created is found in Genesis Chapter 2 verse 21-2 5

21 And the LORD God caused a deep sleep to fall upon Adam, and he slept: and he took one of his ribs, and closed up the flesh instead thereof;22 And the rib, which the LORD God had taken from man, made he a woman, and brought her unto the man.23 And Adam said, This is now bone of my bones, and flesh of my flesh: she shall be called Woman, because she was taken out of Man.

24 Therefore shall a man leave his father and his mother, and shall cleave unto his wife: and they shall be one flesh.

[25] And they were both naked, the man and his wife, and were not ashamed.

We see the institution taken place in the Garden of Eden because of the fall of man Godly marriages has been attacked and the institution of marriage.

We are finding so many people are quick to run out as fast as they ran in, the enemy has been devouring the union by causing others to adhere to his lies and separate or divorce on grounds that can be worked out in some instances they just don't want to give what they are required to give in the relationship.

There are some people that are selfish and they are not concerned about the needs of their spouse this is also why divorce is seen in the Christian family.

In other circumstances there are some people that went through devastated issues in the marriage such as abuse or infidelity, betrayal or the spouse not wanting to be married anymore and walking out on them.

These are very real issues that can cause severe damage and need repair in the soul. Those who endure brokenness and this kind of hardship need the Lord to heal their hearts and help them to pick up the pieces and begin to live again.

God helps those who have gone through this but the ones who only wanted a divorce to get with another person or other selfish purposes are not reasons to leave the marriage union. We see lots of different scenarios that play out in this matter. It is a sad epidemic that needs our attention in order to reconstruct and preserve the Godly union.

However despite this sad epidemic there are mature couples despite facing conflict and hard issues seek Godly wisdom and make a choice to be restored, reconciled and remain together. They learn to work with one another and operate in patience and Gods love. They embrace forgiveness and reconciliation.

Even when there are unresolved issues that are not settled the husband and wife makes the conscious decision they want to fight for their marriage and make the necessary changes in order to realign the relationship. They learn to seek God and depend on him to help their marriage.

God will bless this union because they are seeking his help and as they pray unto him they will learn to grow in their faith and also in their relationship.

Treasure your marriage by cherishing your spouse

It is time to put a high price on the Christian Marriage union again and value the blessing God has allowed you to partake in while living on earth. There are many blessings within the marriage union that God designed for us to receive.

We must live by "what God has joined together let no man put asunder" when we look at this scripture we must acknowledge that God is the one who has joined us together.

When you made the choice to marry your spouse you made the choice to spend the rest of your life with that person God never said you wouldn't face difficult times but the good news is you are facing them together because he has joined you together and he is with you.

Treasure your marriage by cherishing your spouse

Matthew 19:6 Wherefore they are no more twain (two), but one flesh. What therefore God hath joined together, let not man put asunder.

When something is joined it is connected you are unified together, God has connected you together with your spouse that union cannot and shouldn't be easily broken especially if we allow Jesus to be in the center of our marriage he is the joining factor that is needed to sustain the relationship.

Ecclesiastes 4:12 And if one prevail against him, two shall withstand him; and a threefold cord is not quickly broken.

This passage from Ecclesiastes illustrates the importance of Christian companionship. Two Christians that are bound together in Christ are stronger than the individuals themselves.

Treasure your marriage by cherishing your spouse

We believe that Christian marriage is about more than the union of one man and one woman. The Bible teaches us that God performs a miracle in our marriage, uniting us together in a covenant relationship with Him as one.

Treasure your marriage by cherishing your spouse

The Cord of Three Strands is a symbol of that sacred union.

The Cord of Three Strands symbolizes the joining of one man, one woman, and God into a marriage relationship.

Marriage takes three; you, your spouse, and God. It was God who taught us to love. By keeping Him at the center of your marriage, His love will continue to bind you together as one throughout your marriage.

The ring also symbolizes a never-ending circle ~ our marriage should be like the ring although it tarnishes we should never discard it. We can polish it and make it look as good as new. We must always find ways to polish the relationship.

God doesn't want us to view it as broken and ugly he wants us to redefine the beauty of our marriage relationship. That requires great commitment and loyalty from both spouses.

Treasure your marriage by cherishing your spouse

TWO ARE BETTER THAN ONE,
FOR IF ONE FALLS THE OTHER IS THERE.
Two can keep warm when
THE NIGHTS ARE COLD.
Though one may be overpowered,
TWO CAN DEFEND THEMSELVES.
A CORD
OF THREE STRANDS
IS NOT EASILY BROKEN.
ECCLESIASTES 4: 9-12
— *Michaelaevanow.com* —

Treasure your marriage by cherishing your spouse

God does not want us to divorce the marriage relationship by divorcing our spouse. That was not intended for the marriage union because God knew this would cause turmoil and affliction.

It was never intended for the marriage union to be broken because of the horrible effects and damage it causes to the family unit.

This kind of separation damages the physiological, emotional, spiritual and physical wellbeing of the family. We were meant to remain connected as a team, family unit, union.

We must recognize in the marriage relationship we will face difficulties but it is how we handle them that will determine our outcome every time.

Treasure your marriage by cherishing your spouse

I believe experiencing and facing difficulties can strengthen the marriage union but it is how we view the difficulties.

If we are not careful they can also become a stumbling block and hinder the marriage.

If we view these difficulties as a no win situation when we face various adversities it can cause a negative reaction such as wanting to escape or shrink away from the problems or worse each other.

We may be the cause of the negative situation or this adversity can also be caused from an opposing force beyond our control from the evil one. We must learn to identify why we are facing the adversity and who caused it.

Sometimes it is in these adversities we may seek any way to end the frustration of not being able to work out these problems that arise quickly and this can leave us feeling defeated or not wanting to deal with them at all.

 We must identify there are problems we create and problems that are developed out of life situations.

If we learn not to be the problem or create the dysfunction such as (mistrust, infidelity, abuse, disengagement, etc) this list goes on but these listed above are a few examples of self inflicted issues couples can face.

If we can learn how to alleviate the problems we create and deal with the problems that arise from life situations such as (Financial hardship, loss, miscommunication etc) we can work at solving these life situations one by one together.

Treasure your marriage by cherishing your spouse

There is a difference we need to recognize from our created problem verses a life crisis or situation. When we create a problem it is our job to be honest, consult, confess and reveal to our spouse what took place and be able to work through it patiently.

 Hiding or acting like it doesn't exist does more damage to both parties involved. It is better to reveal and expose it no matter how hard it may seem to do.

 The best thing you can do is to release it so you both know what you are dealing with. Then you can pray and release the concern or issue to God in your individual and family prayer time. No one is perfect the sooner we realize this the better we will be! When we assume the role for our spouse to be Mr. Perfect or Mrs. Perfect we place them in a position they can't fulfill and they will fail in this position and fall every time.

We are not to put our spouse or ourselves on a pedestal. Our spouses must also learn not to put us in this position or place us on a pedestal it is damaging, unrealistic and ungodly. We were never meant to worship each other but we were called to love and cherish one another.

We must recognize the frailty of our spouse and ourselves. In our humanness and in our own strength we are fragile so we must continue to rely on Jesus because he is the perfect one he is our Savior and our Strength!

We will fail each other but Jesus will never fail us. When the husband and wife recognizes they are flawed they are actually releasing one another from the bondage of trying to operate in a position of perfection that was never intended for them to operate in. God called the husband and wife to operate in the spirit of Excellence.

There is a difference between excellence and perfection. Excellence means a state of excelling and perfection means the state of being or becoming perfect. God wants us to excel so we should strive towards excelling in our marriage relationship.

However if we place the mandate of perfection on a flawed person we are operating in false hope. This is where we see discouragement or disbelief set in the union at times. We were never intended to put such a high expectancy on our spouse that they can never mess up or fall prey of making mistakes.

Treasure your marriage by cherishing your spouse

We are all subject to letting each other down
and making mistakes on a day to day basis.
Most mistakes are not done intentionally
however because of our imperfections we
experience setbacks and letdowns in the
family.

We are suppose to love unconditionally also
with patience and concern for one another
when we experience this taking place. It is
God who makes us perfect in him and this is
an ongoing work that takes place within our
soul until we get to heaven and receive our
glorified bodies.

We know that there is no good thing that
dwells in our flesh! So it is foolish thinking to
expect a perfect person to show up daily in
the marriage now it is better thinking to
except we are a work in progress and God's
spirit works in us and through us.

Treasure your marriage by cherishing your spouse

This is rational thinking that we must adopt and utilize in the Christian Marriage then our expectations will change and our spouses will not be overwhelmed by our outrageous expectations and we won't be overwhelmed by our spouses.

We must also remember we are striving to be like Jesus and this is a daily journey we are walking on which requires daily surrender and total dependency on Jesus Christ to complete the work he began in us!

This is a process God walks us through! He changes lives we don't change others however we can impact a life but they are the only one that can make the decision and choice to change.

There are many circumstances we may find ourselves in but the issue is not the difficulty of the circumstance,

the issue is how will we both face what we
confront and that reveals our imperfections
but we must show mercy when we encounter
or see behaviors we don't like or understand,
also when we've been hurt by our spouse.

There are times the imperfection reveals
work that needs to take place on the inside of
them. Not that they intentionally meant to
hurt you.

If they are willing to do their work and look
within then we should also be willing to do
our work of forgiveness and forgive. This
same format applies to us.

We all have different struggles but it doesn't
make us better than our spouse if we have
mastered an area they didn't or worse than

our spouse if they mastered an area we are still struggling with. We must show mercy in order to receive mercy, pray for one another.

There are times God will reveal your spouse's shortcoming however he doesn't do this to embarrass him/her but to warn you and also to allow you pray for him/her.

We have to learn how to release, let go and forgive. If we practice this everyday and not hold grudges we become a better unit, better team player.

There are times it is hard to let go of the offense after you experienced hurt but God will give you the strength to do so when you bring the issue to him He wants us to be free and liberated.

When we don't forgive we are actually bound by it because it is holding our hearts captive and we are occupied by the thoughts of that offense.

There are times in a reoccurring hurt you may have to continue to bring that issue to the Lord Jesus and he will grant you peace so anger won't fester in your heart and eventually draw you away from your spouse.

When we are angry it reveals we are experiencing hurt or displeasure. If we are honest we all get angry or upset from time to time if we feel like we've experienced betrayal, felt misused or misunderstood.

Anger is a strong feeling of displeasure, grief, pain or trouble. God warned us to be angry but sin not.

Treasure your marriage by cherishing your spouse

Ephesians 4:26(KJV)Be ye angry, and sin not:
let not the sun go down upon your wrath

This lets us know there are times we will get angry or experience situations that will make us upset but we must choose how we respond to the anger. This is a challenge for many not to react in anger there are times we do well and other times we fall short.

We must practice better reactions in these situations. As we grow in the faith God gives us many tests to work out patience the Holy Spirit will always reveal our struggle and bring conviction to areas we have not mastered.

This reveals we must rely on Jesus and allow the Holy Spirit to guide us by listening and being led.

In the marriage union we must learn how to let go of anger, fits of rage, or uneasiness quickly so it won't burn the marriage relationship and leave it in ashes which leads to unresolved issues.

There are always repairs that need to be done in order to improve and survey the condition of the relationship. So it is the job of the Husband/ Wife to ask God to reveal the positives and negatives within the union and also grant us wisdom and discipline on how to deal with the negatives while continuing to nurture and enrich the positive attributes.

It is always helpful to list what is working, what needs to change after prayerfully seeking God about these areas. You can make a separate list then come together view each other's list and create a new list together.

Treasure your marriage by cherishing your spouse

I pray that your love for each other will overflow more and more, and that you will keep on growing in your knowledge and understanding.
--Philippians 1:9

Treasure your marriage by cherishing your spouse

Do part 1 exercise separately then share what you wrote

Husband

Positive about your Marriage Relationship	Negative about your Marriage Relationship

Wife

Positive about your Marriage Relationship	Negative about your Marriage Relationship

Part 2 – Work on this together after sharing the above

Godly and Healthy Solutions for your Marriage Union

Keep	Throw Out
What works	**What's not working**

This exercise chart can be utilized in many areas of your marriage and it can be done monthly to determine where you are.

After doing this Marriage builder it will help the Husband/Wife get a clear view of what is working in the relationship and what is not working for the team your household.

It also helps you move away from doing the same thing over and over especially if it is not working in your marriage union. This work will begin the work that will move you from dysfunctional relationship to functional.

I call this alleviating clutter throwing out the garbage that causes negative buildup in the relationship. There are a lot of times we tolerate each other's garbage which symbolizes our baggage because we love each other. We sometimes skate around bad attitudes, anger, resentment, in proper communication, we can go on and on about this we accept this because we don't want to step on anyone's toes per say.

There are times we must confront the stench that's been there for months and sometimes years, we must get rid of the garbage clear out all the waste that is damaging the relationship and each other.

When you throw out the negative and begin to practice the new behavior you will begin to feel better because the negative stress of the bad behavior will not be choking the relationship or each other.

You will be able to breathe clearer around each other because you will be more relaxed and the tension will lesson as you are putting new positive behaviors into practice. You will achieve better results and begin to experience the beauty again.

If you cherish each other you will want to do this work, it is not easy work but it will make things a lot better when you continue to do this work once a month or whenever needed. Create a couple meeting place where you both can sit down and discuss issues both positive and negative this will improve communication.

It will allow both people to grow in talking and listening to each other this is a process that takes practice the more you interact and engage in this type of behavior the better results you will achieve.

Here is a key factor that you should always practice tend to the issues of the relationship little by little, this is great wisdom because you can't fix everything all at once it is best to tackle one issue at a time in a loving way. While you are engaging in this work you are actually getting to learn yourself and also your mate.

Treasure your marriage by cherishing your spouse

You are learning what you like and dislike the type of person you are, what you can change or improve and also what you are excelling at. You also learn a lot more about your significant other there likes and dislikes and also their concerns and the type of person they are.

When you experience this you will begin to see the differences as well as the similarities you both share.

This is also valuing what your spouse brings to the relationship. Your spouse should also value what you bring as well. We are not carbon copies of each other. The Husband (Man) brings the treasure God has blessed him with to the wife and the Wife (Woman) brings her treasures that God has blessed her with to the husband.

Treasure your marriage by cherishing your spouse

She is becoming the Proverbs 31 wife striving to be this woman by surrendering herself and allowing God to make her daily.

The Husband is becoming the Godly Husband striving to love her like Jesus loves the Church by surrendering himself to Jesus and learning how to give himself for her and loving her unconditionally.

The Holy Spirit guides the Husband and Wife they learn how to tend to each other's needs not out of obligation but from a place of care and gratitude. They learn how to submit to God and one another by putting their spouse needs before their own needs. They also learn how to improvise and humble themselves. This is the type of servant hood we are called to in the marriage relationship.

Nevertheless let every one of you in particular so love his wife even as himself; and the wife see that she reverence her husband. Ephesians 5:33

God wants us to express our love by taking care of each other and experiencing giving of self on a new level. We are challenged everyday to release this love and compassion to serve our spouse in various capacities.

Treasure your marriage by cherishing your spouse

It takes a lifetime to learn each other because we are always growing and evolving so we must be patient in the getting to know you process.

If truth be told we will never fully know everything about our spouses we will only experience what God reveals to us every day. Our spouse can share with us there inner thoughts and feelings however God is the one who created us and knows everything about us.

We must come to the conclusion we will never fully know everything about our spouse only what is shared and revealed to us. God allows us to experience life with each other and create lasting memories.

Treasure your marriage by cherishing your spouse

Once we are married we will always see new
things, behaviors that were missed in the
beginning when we met our spouse or during
courtship. Of course this will take place
because we are now experiencing new levels
of intimacy we didn't share before marrying
and living with one another.

God calls us into new areas of relating within
the friendship, lover and partner role he
wants us to develop each area throughout the
marriage. When we spend time with and
around each other we learn relation skills.
When we learn how to relate to each other in
these various capacities on a daily basis it will
eventually strengthen the union
tremendously.

Treasure your marriage by cherishing your spouse

"...This is my Beloved,
and this is my Friend..."
SONG OF SOLOMON 5:16

God wants us to develop friendship in the marriage relationship. It is through this friendship which is one level of intimacy we build a bond as we grow closer to one another. When you develop friendship and become each other's best friend it helps the marriage union to flourish.

Friendship in the marriage creates an atmosphere of ease within the relationship, freedom to be self without judgment, and also letting go of trying to put on all of the time. When you operate in friendship you begin to enjoy sharing time, creating moments and enjoying activities with one another.

Two people are not discouraged to be themselves around one another. When your spouse becomes your friend you value and cherish them also in that capacity as well.

Treasure your marriage by cherishing your spouse

Friendship brings balance to the marriage relationship you learn not only to love your spouse but also to like them and not just tolerate them or love from an obligation stand point of view. You enjoy being around them because you see the value they bring to the relationship and to you.

You will also experience the joy of creating beautiful moments together and learn what they enjoy doing by participating in this you will see the variety and value they bring to the union.

One golden rule we must abide by in our relationship is Friendship is developed never forced. We can never force our spouse to be our friend however we can learn how to grow and develop a friendship with them.

This friendship will last over a life time and will always bring understanding to the relationship on many levels throughout all you will ever experience together. If we allow ourselves to embrace and find friendship with in our mate we will discover the blessing this brings to our marriage as a whole.

It is in this friendship communication, care, and great fellowship develops and is nurtured. Throughout the friendship that is developed over a period of time you will learn how to cherish your spouse from the aspect of a friendship point of view as well.

Friendship and being each other's best friend is a beautiful gift God wants us to partake in. This camaraderie has many benefits we can gleam from and its positive fellowship will trickle into other areas of our relationship.

We can only grow stronger from enjoying, sharing and cherishing this type of love.

The early clause of Proverbs17:17 states a friend loves at all times, we must learn to embrace this scripture and put this into practice. No matter what you experience learn to show love all the time.

This is the challenge we must challenge ourselves to put into action. If we are to cherish our spouse we will learn how to love them at all times.

This love will bless us and lead us into the next stage or role of the relationship which is becoming lovers to one another which is another level of intimacy.

There is another level of intimacy of love God gifted us with the joining of the physical body and soul this allows us to share the beauty of being lovers and becoming one!

After we were married and said our vows, this was the beginning of coming together the next stage took place on the honey moon which was the consummating of the marriage.

This gift God gave the union to share our bodies and join the souls is a special bond that each marriage couple shares. It ties the souls together and unites the couple as one. In marriage God reveals his plan for marital bliss.

We must learn how to enjoy what God has blessed us with in Holy Matrimony. We must be comfortable around one another to express our love and learn that love language also.

We must be able to grow together in our intimacy level as well and speak the language we both understand. It is our job to maintain what was created from day one. There will always be changes but we must learn how to be lovers. Lovers share romantic and sexual relationship with one another.

This is what God called us to within the marriage union. He wants us to cherish our spouse and be the lover he is calling us to be.

We must learn to be intentional in this area as well. Lovers go beyond friendship but friendship within the marriage can bring comfortableness and make it easy to flow into becoming great lovers God intended us to be.

Christians tend to run from this topic we know it is sacred and also very personal but it also is the blessing God wants us to

Treasure your marriage by cherishing your spouse

experience within the confinement of the marriage union ordained by God.

The Song of Solomon is a beautiful display of love, romance, beautiful poetry and the gift God intended for the bride and groom growing into husband and wife to share throughout the marriage.

Treasure your marriage by cherishing your spouse

We must redefine lovers and how can we continue to prosper in this role in our union.

In marriage making love or sexual attraction towards one another is a beautiful thing to express and should only be desired among each other. God lets us know the marriage bed is undefiled so we have access to become beautiful lovers in and out of the bedroom.

God uses this for joining husband and wife together and also for procreation to create a child or children in the marriage. Whatever God's will for your marriage should be embraced.

God intended for the marriage union to experience many levels of intimacy within the marriage relationship.

There are many levels God gifted us to share intimacy with each other. He wanted us to experience the joy and love in many ways by sharing and creating beautiful experiences and bonds that are developed from these numerous interactions.

We were suppose to relate to one another by giving ourselves in the act and expression of love in the acts of love making and also sharing various ways also outside the acts of lovemaking.

There are many ways of expression and every couple must learn their ways and rhythm of expressing love towards one another.

Cherishing one another in intimacy reveals a togetherness that needs to transpire among each other only.

There are many love languages and we all speak different languages but the challenge is to learn each other's language and learn to grow to be vulnerable when expressing love. We are challenged to share ourselves on many levels with our spouse and they ought to do the same.

 When we allow others to look within us and really embrace who we are that is Intimacy (<u>In to me see</u>) and this begins the journey of lovers relating there inward feelings outwards.

If you never express what you are feeling within you will never experience the release of giving and sharing with your spouse. You will deprive your spouse of the love he /she needs to receive because you are withdrawn in this area.

Lovers learn to share, express and communicate on many levels. Bringing down walls and barriers is encouraged to become naked before one another to experience the depth of true love and intimacy. This is the binding of hearts that needs to take place, the intertwining of souls that God causes in order to sustain the becoming one and walking in oneness.

When we cherish becoming lovers we also need to adapt the role partner in the relationship.

Partner in marriage is simply a husband and wife our spouse we work together as a team. Partnership is crucial to functioning in a Christian marriage. We must be able to relate to our partner on a day to day basis in order to establish a beautiful relationship.

As partners we become players on the same side we are on the same team. God wants us to know when we decided to get married we signed up on the same team. We are not each other's enemies we are one in togetherness on the same team. In revealing this it goes back to the concept walking in agreement like I explained earlier. We must always recognize the power of agreement and oneness.

When we examine the team concept there are many great players that has many different talents and attributes to offer the team as individuals but as a team there is one goal and purpose and they must be team players. When we look at the marriage relationship we can identify that is it not an individual effort but it is a team effort with the same goals and purpose. God created the marriage union and he intended for the marriage to work as a team and not in singleness.

When we were in our singleness we operated as individuals basically we were viewed as those who play individual sports pretty much a run your own race, and take care of yourself syndrome. When you are married that take care of yourself syndrome becomes take care of each other, what is best for the team not just self.

 So this definitely changes the dynamics of partnership and becoming the God ordained team God wanted your marriage to be. It begins with the partners first and that is the Husband and Wife then your children will follow what you set for the team.

You are never partners with your children you are there parents but you are partners to each other. If you have children they play the team role as well but as a player in the family. So this means they can assist with the vision you and your spouse lay out. They are to walk in obedience to authority not be the authority figures.

Treasure your marriage by cherishing your spouse

So partnership is the establishment of the
family as well. The husband and wife work
hand in hand in every area to create the best
team possible.

God has gifted you both with many talents
you will use throughout the marriage to build
a great team and union together.

Your job is to tap into what he has placed
inside of you and to work together in
harmony greater than you collide and fall
apart.

We can say partnership in the marriage is
pulling together to work towards the same
cause. The vision of the house must be
defined, revisited and carried out. It must
also be cherished and valued. If you don't
value your partner you won't value your
team which is your marriage.

Becoming partners is another level of intimacy we must learn how to operate in. You grow into partnership over the years once your friendship is developed and you become lovers you flow into partnership as well.

Partnership allows you to work together which means tackling anything in the relationship pertaining to things in the home, outside the home, business decisions, family decisions, financial obligations and decisions etc.

This is why there is no time for separation, selfishness and stubbornness to be the driving force of the relationship. In a partnership there is the meeting of the minds and a coming together to work in a cohesive fashion that will bring positive impact to the team!

Treasure your marriage by cherishing your spouse

If we cherish our spouse then we will by any means necessary surrender our will and seek Gods will for our marriage.

We don't work against the grain to cause confusion, we don't drive at the same time, we don't run the train off the tracks because we can't get our way or don't understand the vision.

In a Christian marriage we walk in submission to Jesus Christ, each other and serve on the team. We don't sit out on the sidelines when we are supposed to pitch in and give of ourselves. We learn to help one another function within the partnership role. Operating in the friendship, lover and partnership role will greatly enhance our union.

When we cherish our spouse and receive them as friend, lover and partner and also become these three things to them there is closeness a net that is fitly joined around the husband and wife.

That net is not easily broken no matter what you will face over the course of the marriage relationship. You will continue to grow stronger and prosper.

If you learn how to yield to God's will for your relationship. If you obey his will for your marriage relationship you will prosper no matter what you will experience.

 You will see God's hand in your relationship when you recognize he was the one keeping you together. You will begin to see your marriage in a new light because his mercy extended his hand of grace towards you and your spouse. You will see a beautiful marriage and value it as a precious gift that is to be treasured in this lifetime.

Treasure your marriage by cherishing your spouse

The Godly marriage is a beautiful gift from God and it allows you to give, receive love and share your treasures with the one you are joined to and that is your soul mate, best friend, lover, partner and your spouse. When you learn to cherish the spouse God gave you, you are actually being grateful to God for what he allowed you to experience.

Every day you wake up to your spouse is a new day God has given to experience his love and in return release it to your spouse.

There are many great moments we can create if we see the value our spouse brings to the union and also if we recognize the value we bring and give.

In the marriage relationship we are designed to build ~ what we build is determined by us. The choices we make to build or tear down will determine what type of marriage we desire to have and live with. We have a daily choice to build a positive or negative atmosphere with in the relationship which will affect the team in a positive or negative way.

We are suppose to add to the life of our spouse what we add is up to us. We can't make anyone happy that would be a form of control and also a hard task we could never accomplish. To be happy means to be pleased and we can never fulfill that because our spouse's desires and emotions are always changing.

That is not our job our job or task is to add happiness to the lives of others not make anyone happy. There is a difference. Happiness is an emotion felt within we don't control anyone's emotions but we can share

Treasure your marriage by cherishing your spouse

joyful moments that can create an atmosphere of happiness to flow.

There are many ways we express ourselves so we are never responsible for the response of others we are responsible for our own response.

To always be glad is a state of mind, there are naturally happy people while others are the opposite and that person might be difficult to please. Because desires are always changing we must come to the conclusion we can never please our spouse. That was not intended for us to do.

We must learn how to please God then seek wisdom on how to relate to our mate again that takes learning the person there likes and dislikes and growing together.

Treasure your marriage by cherishing your spouse

There is a difference between pleasing and relating to someone with that said we can make the decision to add life or we can add stress, add joy to the relationship or frustration add encouragement or discouragement. We can add assistance or add discontentment in the relationship. It is better to add positive attributes and subtract the negative pressures we can bring if we are not careful.

If we are truthful we can say there were times we all brought both positive and negative into the relationship from time to time but our **goal is to add more positive behaviors than negative.**

The positive behaviors will always be welcomed and increase love in the atmosphere, in your heart and the heart of your spouse on the other hand to much of the negative behaviors can choke the life out of the relationship and cause pain and damage to your heart and the heart of your spouse.

God is calling us to extend what he has given to us to our spouse he wants us to share his love and kindness. If we come to the conclusion that we will allow God to love through us every day we will be the giver of Gods attributes and the marriage will blossom because we are the first partakers of God's grace and his love.

We can't wait for our spouse to do this first we must learn how to do this work first if we are changed the change will be seen.

If both people are doing this work then change will be evident on both parts. The marriage union will become stronger and better.

God wants us to be faithful, loyal, understanding and committed to our spouse and that is how we cherish them by releasing this love to them after all God is faithful, loyal, understanding and committed to us. He teaches us how to be like him and give these gifts to our mates.

Loyalty

LOYALTY MAKES A PERSON ATTRACTIVE.
PROVERBS 19:22

Treasure your marriage by cherishing your spouse

~ Treasure Your Marriage Prayer ~

Lord help us to remember the day we met how often we sometimes forget the day you allowed us to unite together in Holy Matrimony we said our vows in front of family and friends as we were turned toward each other holding hands and praying for your blessings as we exchanged wedding bands. Help us to remember what we shared while we show each other how much we really care.

Lord help us to remember the day we met how often we sometimes forget when we said our I do's which echoed through the room. Lord help us to remember the love we shared then and grow within us your love that is so dear. We thank you for your many blessings you bestow over us.

Treasure your marriage by cherishing your spouse

God bless this marriage
with Hope that is sure,
with Faith that is steady,
and *Love*

that endures.

Treasure your marriage by cherishing your spouse

When something is priceless you cherish the value of it you esteem it highly. It is time for us to esteem each other and put our spouses back in the place of being valued by knowing his/her worth. When we view the marriage relationship as priceless then we acknowledge there is no price we will not be willing to pay because this relationship is worth the value of being treasured.

When you purchase something of great value you take special care of it because of it's worth, it is costly and you don't want to damage or discard it this is the same way we should view and treat our relationship! Take great care of it.

In order to cherish our spouse we must define what is the real meaning of love?

As Christians we are to model the biblical meaning of love and that is found in 1

Treasure your marriage by cherishing your spouse

Corinthians 13:4- 8 this passage of scripture spells out and defines the meaning of Love and reveals what it is and what it is not.

This is the defining model God wants us to pattern the way we treat others after. When we discover what God's love looks like then we will be able to see what needs to be developed within us. In order to be a loving spouse we must grasp this concept of God's teaching on love! If we learn what love is then we will be able to put into practice its attributes.

When we learn what love is not then we will be able to do away with what was practiced in error. We can also identify quickly the behaviors that are not representing this kind of love.

God calls us into a love relationship with him and also our spouse. He calls and causes us to love because he is love and we experience his love first.

Because he drew us to him with love and kindness in return we are suppose to share that love we received with others. Love is put into action. When we love our spouse we are revealing the love with the actions we portray.

1 Corinthians13:4 opens up with Love is Patient and kind this lets us know what love is. In order to show love to our spouse we must be patient and kind. This means we must practice and get into the habit of putting on being patient and kind towards them. To be patient means to be calm, diligent and understanding. To be kind

means to be helpful being a loving person. When this is revealed to us we must understand we can't do this in our own strength.

We need the aide of the Holy Spirit to be taught and to practice how we ought to put on this love that will be relayed to our spouse. This is why it is important for us to really examine what love is and what kind of love God is calling us into. Once this is revealed to us then we can learn how to operate and function in this type of love which is Gods truth and true love. This is the unconditional love God is bringing us into and want to activate within us.

We must do away with old traditions, concepts or precepts that we were taught and what doesn't line up with the word of God.

Once we do this we can begin to see the truth, accept truth and walk in truth. This is the love God wants us to embrace the patient and kind love that we experience from him. This is the love we are encouraged to release to our spouse.

God wants us to cherish our spouse so he gives us principles of what love is and what love is not. He defines now what love is not and if we find ourselves behaving in these false attributes of love we can make the necessary changes to eliminate those behaviors that are listed here.

There is a process of elimination that must take place within the old man we must go through a transformation of thought and behavior in order for us not to function in what love is not. As we continue to view 1 Corinthians 13 we see God reveals what love is not he says love is not jealous; love does not brag and is not arrogant, It does not dishonor others, it is not self-seeking, it is not easily angered, it keeps no record of wrongs.

 When we view this definition of love in the marriage relationship we can see how we should conduct ourselves.

We can come to the conclusion that this is God's standard of love that we ought to measure how we need to treat our spouse and also how they need to treat us. Once we recognize this we become more aware of what we need to continue to practice and also what treatments we are practicing that needs to change because it is not lining up with this love definition which is God's love and his recipe for a beautiful marriage one that is flowing in his design and purpose.

Treasure your marriage by cherishing your spouse

is patient & kind
DOES NOT ENVY OR BOAST
IT IS NOT PROUD OR RUDE
not self-seeking or easily angered

keeps no record of wrongs it does not delight in evil
REJOICES WITH TRUTH
always protects & trusts
hopes and perseveres
LOVE NEVER FAILS

If we can view this passage as the model of love that we want our union to experience then we will be eager to learn and understand how to move and operate in this LOVE in the marriage relationship. There are many lessons we learn about love and this godly lesson teaches us how to embrace what love is and to do away with what love is not.

If we continue to walk in what love is not then we will never benefit from what love really is. Love never fails love is the gift that keeps on giving so we are the vessels that must decide to love and when we make this decision on a day to day basis we are choosing to be like God because God is love.

If we are talking about cherishing our spouses then in order for us to cherish him/her we must admit that loving them is the only way to do so.

If we don't love them then we will not be able to cherish, respect, show mercy or grace towards them. However if we are professing our love for them then we must adapt to the biblical meaning of Love found in 1 Corinthians 13.

Because we are born again we are also learning how to be more Christ like that is why we must embrace patience in our union because we are still learning how to operate in God's love and also in the fruits of the spirit. We are beginning to walk in understanding and what does this look like within the marriage relationship. We must be taught and be developed in this new way of living.

We must learn to adapt ourselves to the teaching of God's word. Once we begin to do this and humble ourselves and pray and seek God for guidance and assistance then we will be able to implement this into our daily interaction with the one we cherish.

When we make the conscious decision to transform those areas that needs transformation then we are expressing our love towards our spouse. Let us learn to be patient with this process and also understand if we are willing to see where we need to change that is the beginning of beautification of self and also the marriage relationship.

When we accept the beautification process then we are accepting to love and cherish our spouse. Transformation is continuous in the marriage relationship and this work should always be valued.

When you learn to cherish your spouse then you are not bothered by the necessary changes needing to take place within and also in the relationship.

We learn to embrace this work and put into practice principles that will help us become disciplined in love.

Eventually this also helps us in our individual walk with the Lord where we learn obedience and also how to receive correction and embrace godly living.

God is calling us to walk in love together and as we do this on a daily basis we will grow closer together as God's reflection will be seen in us and also in our relationship. His glory will be revealed in us and also in our marriage union as we learn to embrace and cherish one another.

There is great pleasure and blessings that God gives your union when you partake in walking in a disciplined love and practice loving one another from this perspective.

Treasure your marriage by cherishing your spouse

Ten ways to love

Listen without interrupting. (Proverbs 18)
Speak without accusing. (James 1:19)
Give without sparing. (Proverbs 21:26)
Pray without ceasing. (Colossians 1:9)
Answer without arguing. (Proverbs 17:1)
Share without pretending. (Ephesians 4:15)
Enjoy without complaint. (Philippians 2:14)
Trust without wavering. (1 Corinthians 13:7)
Forgive without punishing. (Colossians 3:13)
Promise without forgetting. (Proverbs 13:12)

Treasure your marriage by cherishing your spouse

God wants us to treasure our marriage and cherish our spouse by praying when we learn how to pray for ourselves and our mate we will experience transformation.

We will learn how to see the marriage the way God see's it and also we will learn how to receive instructions from the Lord Jesus on how to operate in the marriage on a daily basis. If we allow the Holy Spirit to guide us and teach us then we will walk in greater victory.

We must learn how to be slow to speak and quick to hear if we want to cherish and value our spouse and our marriage. There are a lot of great principles we can apply to our marriage from the word of God.

If we learn how to apply what we read or study from the word of God and continue to practice these principles we will experience greater victories.

We are challenged as believers first to put into practice the teachings of the Bible and when we conform to this and not fight against it then we will experience peace and also greater understanding within the union. We will also have a greater appreciation for our spouse.

 When we adapt to married life then we will produce good fruits in that marriage. The good fruit that is yielded will manifest blessings that will cause the union to prosper.

However when we don't conform and fight against the adapting process we will only produce bad fruit. The bad fruit is the rotten behaviors that will cause the union to deteriorate.

If we say we cherish our spouse and our marriage relationship then we would want to do everything we possibly can to cause the relationship to flourish and not deteriorate.

If we see any sign of deterioration then we would want to address it before it does greater damage. If we cherish our marriage then we ought to be diligent in the repairing process.

God is calling us and causing us to pay greater attention to the family unit we are suppose to be good stewards over what God blessed us with. This not only pertains to financial blessings but to all that concerns us. We must guard our marriage and care for it. We must learn how to maintain it by taking care of it.

If we are going to cherish our spouse and treasure our marriage then we must be aware of the necessary development that needs to take place.

We can't allow turbulence and opposition to overtake the marriage relationship. We must learn how to engage in much prayer we ought to pray without ceasing.

There is one thing that changes climates and atmospheres in your marriage union and that is prayer. God uses prayer as a vehicle for you to have access to Him. It is in that prayer time you can release all concerns, repent, worship and praise God and in return you will receive instruction from him through the Holy Spirit and you will also receive comfort, strength, correction, understanding and God's wisdom.

Prayer also helps transform you and it reveals you, releases, restores, revitalize, it also opens up your heart to the leading of the

Holy Spirit and for you to experience renewal in your thinking.

If you really want to show love to your spouse pray for them and also for your marriage. By doing this you are allowing God to work and move within your family.

Praying for yourself, your spouse and your marriage draws you closer to him/her and you begin to see what God reveals, your thinking will not be distorted and you begin to accept what you cannot change and allow God's will to be done in your marriage relationship.

When you are committed to praying you are learning how to cherish your spouse. You will have a greater level of compassion and mercy towards your family.

Treasure your marriage by cherishing your spouse

You will experience a new level of commitment to your covenant no matter what you may experience. You will also learn how to release the unresolved issues to the Lord Jesus and let him touch your heart and your spouse's heart. God can do what we can't do.

We must always remember God created us he knows how to work in us and on us. Sometimes we walk in era because we want to assist God in the process of getting our spouse attention but the Holy Spirit knows how to draw us unto him and He knows exactly what we need. He knows what our union needs and we have to walk in faith and believe our prayers are being answered.

We must believe God is able to move on the hearts of men and he is the one by the leading of the Holy Spirit that takes away the stony heart and gives a heart of flesh. He does this in us and also in our spouse. We must let God be God in our home and allow the Holy Spirit to assist us in every area of our life. We are called into the marriage union to give and release the love God placed within us.

The cherishing is evident and revealed when we acknowledge we care and love our spouse.

We are challenged by God to be diligent and be on purpose with showing care and concern about our spouse and the marriage relationship.

We must be committed with a passion which will cause us to be persistent and on purpose in sharing our heart and our self with our mate.

Treasure your marriage by cherishing your spouse

We will not be persuaded to leave but
convinced to remain and pour into our
spouse and the marriage relationship what
God has poured into us. God never gave us
the mind to quit or opt out when we didn't
want to give of our selves anymore.

Jesus gave us the ability to endure and he has
given us life and an abundant life in Him.

So this lets us know there is an abundance of
love flowing on the inside of us but
somewhere we got confused and thought we
can give when we feel conducive to give and
show love only when it benefits us but we
didn't recognize there is an abundance of
overflow that is suppose to flow through us
daily.

Treasure your marriage by cherishing your spouse

There is no shortage of God's love and because he has given us His love we must release what we have received. If we pick and choose when to release love then we are being bias in our giving.

 If we are to cherish our spouse then there is no place for being bias or stingy with what we have received freely from the Lord Jesus and that is his love. We are challenged to embrace love and give love even in times that are not always favorable.

If we want to have and experience a beautiful marriage then we must be the first participants and recipients of receiving God's love and releasing His love. We must recognize it is crucial to establish a loving relationship if we are to cherish our spouse.

God wants us to experience his fullness of joy and in order to do that we must learn to understand what we are called to be in the marriage relationship. We are called away from single mindedness and into oneness. We are called away from old behaviors that are not bringing God glory. We are called to unite and to live amongst one another in peace and in unity. We are called into a love fellowship, love relationship, a love that abides and abounds, a love that resides and fulfills, a love that endures and lasts, because love quenches the soul, love carries, love covers, love embraces, love never fails.

We must accept the challenge to love again from the place of a purified heart. When we love from a place of a purified heart we are not filled with pride or our own self seeking selfish ways we allow God to love through us and we accept his ways of releasing love and this is where God can truly restore the marriage.

This is a place where contamination must be rid from the heart. If we allow the contamination to remain then that is what is hindering the heart from giving pure love.

We must have God's desires within us and His desire is that we release Love. Love is the greatest gift of all. It is the greatest gift we can give our spouse. It is also the greatest gift we can receive.

If we build our relationship on love which is a Godly attribute then we will ultimately be able to experience the blessings of that fruit we are operating in. Love is one of the fruits of the spirit and we must be able to flow freely in this gift in order to see transformation and achieve great results within the relationship.

When we put on love we are choosing to be governed by what love is so we then begin to operate in patience, kindness and endurance.

We develop in ourselves a better sense of learning how to operate in this love. We acknowledge and recognize we must practice and be disciplined in this type of love.

If we are committed to practicing love then we will reap the rewards of seeing love being carried out in the relationship. Our behaviors will mimic how we want to be treated, and we will learn to release what we want to receive because in actuality we can train ourselves to behave and adapt to new ways of how we deal with our spouse.

If we say we want to cherish them then we must be concerned about what message we are conveying to them. We can say one thing and live out another. We must show them

Treasure your marriage by cherishing your spouse

through our actions in word and also in deed,
and they must also do the same towards us.
This is the daily challenge we will always
face.

Choosing to love in word and also in deed or
behaving rotten and developing a negative
atmosphere due to the choices we make.

Once we understand we can make better
choices and decisions when it comes to
learning to love and enjoy our spouse by
cherishing them then we will learn how to
address any negativity within or those that
plague the relationship.

 We can cancel these assignation assignments
by taking captive our thoughts and bringing
our self under subjection to the Spirit of
Jesus Christ that is within us.

This takes an identification of who is the real enemy and foe. It also causes us to come to grip that we need to do self evaluation on a normal basis to understand where we are and what we need to release and rid ourselves of.

In the marriage relationship we must rid ourselves of all Pride because the bible lets us know in proverbs 16:18 that pride goes before destruction and a haughty spirit before a fall.

In the book of James 4:6 lets us know that God resists the proud and gives grace to the humble.

If we are prideful we will never be able to admit our shortcomings and we will always point the finger at others.

Treasure your marriage by cherishing your spouse

If we are prideful we will walk around with an (I) syndrome always focused on me only. If we are humbled we will always be quick to identify the faults in us and be willing to work on them. We will also receive grace from the Lord because we know His strength is made perfect in our weakness.

Jesus will grace us with his love and his spirit will guide us while showing us an excellent way. This will cause us to embrace improvement that will take place because we will learn to acknowledge we need to grow and improve daily.

However if we operate in pride and never admit our flaw area's what a disservice we will do to our self, our spouse and our marriage relationship.

Treasure your marriage by cherishing your spouse

So again let me reiterate the work begins in us and if we care about our spouse then we will care about our own disposition and how we are to work on the transforming process then the transformation will be revealed and received by our spouse.

There are many stages of growth that is required for the marriage relationship to mature and become developed. Just as the caterpillar becomes a butterfly in various stages the same can be viewed in us and also in the marriage relationship.

When the caterpillar is in the cocoon that is the crucial stage of development whether the caterpillar will transform into the beautiful butterfly will determine how development occurs.

Treasure your marriage by cherishing your spouse

This can also be an example of the work that takes place in the first few stages of the marriage union. The first few years of marriage are the nesting stage and also the learning stage of who you actually married. It is in these first few years you will learn how to adapt and build. There will be an adaptation process that is necessary to develop.

How can we develop if we don't adapt. If we don't learn how to adapt then we will never be ready to build. We must come to terms that if we are not cherishing our spouse could it be we have not adapted to this relationship instead we have forgotten we were supposed to be developing a life together with them.

Loving our spouse means growing together in love.

Treasure your marriage by cherishing your spouse

When we are growing together we experience development. To develop means to bring out the capabilities or possibilities of, to cause to grow or expand.

God has called us into the marriage union to develop and build together. If we cannot first develop then how can we build? We must first come to the conclusion that we cannot despise the development process and that is what we are experiencing in the marriage relationship.

We cannot fret because we don't like to experience the pain or transition when we are being stretched during the adaption and development stage.

God is using this development stage to make us one when we learn to yield to this then we will understand this is the preparation that

Treasure your marriage by cherishing your spouse

is necessary for us to endure in order to usher us into the building stage of the marriage relationship.

We cannot bypass this and we cannot get sidetrack when we experience this actually happening in the marriage. Some have run away before the development stage was done and the building never had a chance to occur.

You can't build where there is no foundation. In the development process the foundation is laid. It takes years to build on the foundation that is set and it is in this the marriage relationship growth will never end.

We are not to despise this growth process and we are called by God into this union when we chose to marry our mate. We must allow each other to grow, grow within and also grow together.

Treasure your marriage by cherishing your spouse

We were never called to grow apart and if that is happening we need to evaluate why that is occurring.

Difference of opinion is allowed because we do sometimes have difference of opinion however we were never suppose to allow those opinions or different ways of doing things to separate us and distance us from our spouse.

This is where the growing and learning each other is crucial to bringing greater understanding and a greater level of maturity that will determine how we develop together on a day to day basis which will lead to a month to month interaction eventually moving into years.

Treasure your marriage by cherishing your spouse

We must be willing to grow and allow growth to take place within our spouse if we are going to cherish them.

We can't expect them to come into the marriage perfect, not flawed, knowing everything, because we also are not perfect, we are flawed and we don't know everything. This is a place of learning, treading and charting on new territory.

With that said we must allow liberty and exercise love and not be judgmental when error is evident due to the developing that needs to take place. In the marriage union there will be lots of teachable moments on both ends, we will always learn ourselves and our spouse. We will grasp new ideas, educate ourselves, experience a new way of doing

Treasure your marriage by cherishing your spouse

things and develop creative ways to relate to one another.

We are called to expand in the relationship. To love is to grow if you love your spouse then you want them to grow and become better and also wiser. The same applies to you if they love you also.

We are challenged to become better, our relationship is challenged to grow and expand. The love that we share is meant to grow but it doesn't grow on its own. We grow our love by growing in love. Our love is developed. Our love is tried through the tests we experience. If we become bitter while we are experiencing our couple's testing then we become stagnated in giving the love that is desired to be received.

Treasure your marriage by cherishing your spouse

We must learn to be solid in loving one another and also in our relationship. Stability comes from the marriage relationship becoming solid as a rock and durable.

A durable marriage doesn't mean a problem free marriage however it is a relationship that endures the obstacles that comes with the development process and it learns how to build safe boundaries which protects and prepares for whatever storms they may experience.

They learn to anchor themselves in Christ Jesus when they visit rocky territory and they ride the waves of life's circumstance together. They learn to wither the storm that blows from time to time and learn how to adjust and work together.

Treasure your marriage by cherishing your spouse

They don't allow the storms of life to devour their marriage relationship. However they learn to navigate and maneuver through the rough currents while they also enjoy the smooth sailing as they experience life together.

The durable marriage union rides the tides as they learn how to build on a lasting love relationship.

If we are to cherish our spouse we would want to build with them. The marriage cannot be built by one person's participation and input only. This relationship takes both people's participation and undivided attention.

We must learn to allow God to build our marriage. We must also work at building the relationship.

Treasure your marriage by cherishing your spouse

 When we participate in the building process
we are committed to constantly working on
our self and also the relationship. Building
the marriage relationship consists of building
trust, proper communication, understanding,
exercising love, esteeming each other.

There are so many tools needed to build and
if we cherish our spouse and treasure the
marriage union then we will want to do the
building that is necessary to promote growth
in the relationship.

We will be building for years upon the
foundation that was developed. The growth
process is a never ending process because we
are always grasping and learning one another
and how to relate within the relationship. We
must experience growth and this growth will
be evident and beneficial to have a productive
relationship.

Treasure your marriage by cherishing your spouse

If we never grow we will remain underdeveloped. The same concept can be viewed for the marriage relationship it can be stagnated and underdeveloped if not tended to.

We must make a conscious decision to nurture this relationship if we ought to cherish our spouse and treasure our marriage.

In the marriage we should never get tired of building and redeveloping the family unit because it is one of the greatest institutions we can ever invest in. When we learn to work at the building process then we are ready to show up to the marriage.

Some showed up for the wedding ceremony but forgot to show up and participate in the marriage which is the building process that

T reasure your marriage by cherishing your spouse

takes place every day. We can't only enjoy the perks of the wedding and the title of being husband and wife and not want to experience all that comes with being married. There is a work that needs to be cultivated in the union.

In the union we must be the first participants to establish, undergird, utilize, and encourage the building process. If we are not constantly building within the union will decay on the surface and it will be noticeable. When you don't practice upkeep there is a danger that everything you built will begin to fall apart and become damaged. This can destroy the building.

If we are to cherish our spouse and treasure the marriage relationship then there must be a sense of urgency to want to build correctly and maintain what you built together that is

Treasure your marriage by cherishing your spouse

the upkeep that is necessary to sustain the
relationship from unraveling.

If you don't like what you built together you
can break down the walls and start all over
again to beautify your relationship.

That is the blessing of working together to
create greater concepts and also to design
what is best for your relationship through the
leading of the Holy Spirit you can create
again. The relationship doesn't have to stay
in a destroyed state. It can be revived and
restored again.

You can change what is not working that is
the maintenance that you are encouraged to
partake in. In order to revamp and create
better structure and stability in the union this
is the reconstruction that is necessary for
restoration to occur.

Treasure your marriage by cherishing your spouse

When something is reconstructing it is being redeveloped again in order to become fixed and when it is fixed it serves a better purpose. Our union serves better purpose when it is tended to and is repaired.

The brokenness will be mended and we are able to function at a greater capacity.

God wants the marriage relationship to function at a greater capacity of love, forgiveness, care, trust, faithfulness, fulfillment and purpose that is what we are to work on. Building a relationship that will constantly stand strong together no matter what opposition we will have to face.

When you treasure your marriage by cherishing your spouse you will begin to find the hidden treasure as you develop, build,

T reasure your marriage by cherishing your spouse

and grow together while exploring one another and learning to value the person God made you and also to value the spouse God gave you. You will learn to give in exchange the love you received from the Lord Jesus.

It is time to regain your position and posture in the union and work towards the greater goal to develop together what God placed inside the both of you the hidden treasure that must be developed every day and given to one another in a special way.

Cherish the love you share, cherish the times you are near, draw closer to the gift you received thank God for the times you are able to embrace and retrace, capture the love he bestowed upon your union.

Never let the relationship go it is a treasure that only you can hold.

Treasure your marriage by cherishing your spouse

As you open it up and look inside remember this was the gift your prayers released open it up with caution and never take it for granted.

It is very delicate yet beautiful the heart that he has trusted and given you to love.

Be careful how you handle it because it is hard to get back once it has been discarded. Always cherish your spouse whom God gave you to love. The spouse you received from Heaven above.

I challenge you to grow in love and stand in the love you are called to share with your spouse in the Christian union where God ordained as the institution of Marriage. Your marriage relationship is one of the greatest gifts you can ever receive and you must continue to guard it, treasure it as you learn to cherish your spouse always.

Treasure your marriage by cherishing your spouse

In closing I will say it was a pleasure writing to all those who will read this book and to give a friendly reminder that there are hidden treasures in your marriage and they will be revealed as you learn to see the value in your own marriage relationship by learning how to cherish your spouse.

You are the only one who will begin to see the hidden treasures that lies within your own relationship. Once you begin to develop yourself to find the beauty that lies within your spouse and yourself you will be able to understand the value of your marriage.

Learning the lessons of maintaining, caring and keeping the gift God has blessed you with will allow you to esteem it highly and never discard it.

Treasure your marriage by cherishing your spouse

The greatest gift you can give is love.
Continue to grow in love with your spouse as
God intended you to do. May you learn to
love unconditionally as you treasure your
union and remain loyal!

For where your
Treasure is,
there will your
Heart
be also.
~Matthew 6:21

Treasure your marriage by cherishing your spouse

COVENANT MARRIAGE

IS GOD ORDAINED

Treasure your marriage by cherishing your spouse

Our Marriage Mission

TO HAVE A CHRIST-CENTERED
MARRIAGE THAT BRINGS GLORY
TO GOD THROUGH THE WAY
THAT WE LOVE AND THE WAY
THAT WE LIVE.

THAT WE WOULD BE SERVANTS
OF GRACE WHO GIVE MORE
THAN WE'RE GIVEN
AND FORGIVE BEFORE
WE'RE FORGIVEN.

BE FAITHFUL

REMAIN

Committed to your Commitment!

Stand In Love with your Spouse!

Treasure your marriage by cherishing your spouse

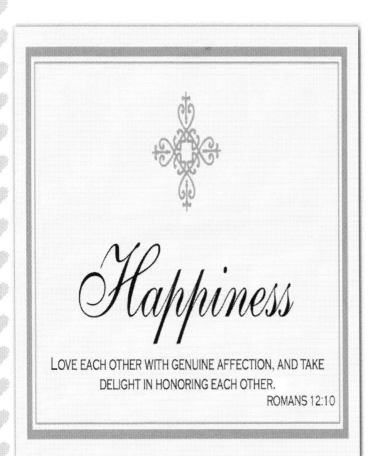

Happiness

LOVE EACH OTHER WITH GENUINE AFFECTION, AND TAKE
DELIGHT IN HONORING EACH OTHER.

ROMANS 12:10

Treasure your marriage by cherishing your spouse

I want my life and my marriage to look less like the world and more like Christ.

T reasure your marriage by cherishing your spouse

~About the Author~

Suzanne E. Uzzell was inspired to write this book to encourage

the Christian Marriage relationship to treasure their relationship by cherishing their spouse. Finding the hidden treasure and what is valuable within them and their spouse will transform the marriage union.

Suzanne is an Ordained Evangelist who is concerned about souls. She ministers where ever God sends her. She is blessed to minister and witness to people from all walks of life. She loves to serve, help and give to others.

She is also an Air force spouse who is married to her loving Husband TSgt Jahi J. Uzzell. Suzanne was privileged to live in various places such as England, Hawaii and the Netherlands she now resides in Las Vegas Nevada on Nellis AFB.

Suzanne is a Native New Yorker who graduated from Herbert H. Lehman College with a B.A. She is an Entrepreneur who enjoys being creative and writing. Treasure your Marriage by Cherishing your spouse is her Fourth book written and Published. Other books she has written are Reach Out and Touch, Chosen Words and Words 2 Ignite the Soul. These books can be found online at Amazon, Barnes & Noble and Lulu.com.

Feel free to follow her Face book page WORDS 4 THE SOUL~ you can get more information on all books and follow the Author!

~ Notes ~

Made in the USA
Middletown, DE
23 March 2022

63089351R00093